The Life and World of

ARISTOTLE

Brian Williams

Heinemann LIBRARY

H www.heinemann.co.uk/library
Visit our website to find out more information about Heinemann Library books.

To order:
☎ Phone 44 (0) 1865 888066
▤ Send a fax to 44 (0) 1865 314091
▭ Visit the Heinemann Library Bookshop at www.heinemann.co.uk/library to browse our catalogue and order online.

First published in Great Britain by Heinemann Library,
Halley Court, Jordan Hill, Oxford OX2 8EJ
a division of Reed Educational and Professional Publishing Ltd.
Heinemann is a registered trademark of Reed Educational & Professional Publishing Ltd.

OXFORD MELBOURNE AUCKLAND
JOHANNESBURG BLANTYRE GABORONE
IBADAN PORTSMOUTH (NH) USA CHICAGO

Designed by Celia Floyd
Illustrated by Jeff Edwards and Joanna Brooker
Originated by Ambassador Litho Ltd
Printed by Wing King Tong in Hong Kong.

ISBN 0 431 14765 5
06 05 04 03 02
10 9 8 7 6 5 4 3 2 1

Northamptonshire Libraries & Information Service	
Peters	08-Aug-02
185	£10.50

Acknowledgements

The Publishers would like to thank the following for permission to reproduce photographs: AKG: p14; Ancient Art and Architecture: pp6, 10, 18, 25, 28; The Art Archive: pp4, 7, 8, 11, 12, 13, 17, 20, 23, 24, 26, 29; British Museum: pp9, 22; Corbis: p15; Scala: pp16, 19; The Travel Library: p27; University of Manchester: p21.

Cover photograph reproduced with permission of The Art Archive.

Our thanks to Rebecca Vickers for her comments during the preparation of this book.

Every effort has been made to contact copyright holders of any material reproduced in this book. Any omissions will be rectified in subsequent printings if notice is given to the Publisher.

Contents

Any words appearing in the text in bold, **like this**, are explained in the glossary.

A land of gods and thinkers

Aristotle of Greece was one of the greatest thinkers who ever lived. Although he was born more than 2300 years ago, his ideas are still talked about today. Perhaps more than any other person, Aristotle's ideas helped shape Western **civilization**.

Aristotle was one of the most important **philosophers** (thinkers) of Ancient Greece. Greek philosophers asked questions such as 'What is true?' and 'What is the best form of **government**?' Aristotle was one of the first scientists to study animals and plants closely, but he was just as interested in how countries are governed, art, religion, and the way we think. He was a teacher too. His most famous pupil was Alexander the Great, one of the greatest **conquerors** in history.

Aristotle's Greece

Aristotle's Greece was the birthplace of **democracy** – the form of 'government by the people' used in many countries today. Ancient Greece was a collection of small city-states. Each city-state had its own government and ruled the villages, farms and ports in the surrounding area. The Greeks had many gods. Every town had temples and statues to these gods who, people believed, looked down on Greece from Mount Olympus.

◄ Greek sculptors made **busts** and statues of famous people. This is a Roman copy of a bust of Aristotle.

Because Greece had little good farmland, many people left to settle in **colonies**. They travelled by ship along the coasts of the Mediterranean Sea. In this way, Greek ideas had spread to North Africa, Italy and Spain.

Aristotle spent many years in Athens, a city famous for its **politicians**, writers and teachers. He wrote in Greek, but his writings were later copied into other languages, and studied by people in many countries. For hundreds of years, people thought Aristotle was right about practically everything. Modern science has shown that, as a scientist, Aristotle was sometimes wrong. Yet he left so many important ideas that people still want to read what he had to say.

▲ Greece is a peninsula – a piece of land sticking out into the sea – surrounded by many islands. Aristotle was born in northern Greece, at Stagira, but spent much of his time in Athens, Asia Minor and the island of Lesbos. He died at Chalcis.

Key dates

400s BC   'Golden Age' in Greece; Pericles leads Athens

384 BC   Aristotle is born

367 BC   Aristotle travels to Athens to study with Plato

344 BC   Aristotle studies nature on the island of Lesbos

336 BC   Alexander becomes king of Greece

335 BC   Aristotle opens the Lyceum in Athens

322 BC   Aristotle dies

Watch the dates

Dates before Christ's birth are often written as 'BC', and the years are counted back towards zero (the date of his birth). After this they go forwards, starting with 1 AD.

A doctor's son

Aristotle was born in 384 BC in the small town of Stagira, on the northwest shore of the Aegean Sea. Stagira had been founded as a **colony** by Ionians, from southern Greece. Aristotle's mother came from Chalcis, on the island of Euboea. His father, Nicomachus, was a doctor and **court physician** to King Amyntas II of Macedonia, a kingdom in the north of Greece. Southern Greeks thought mountainous Macedonia was a wild and uncivilized place.

Welcoming a son

Nicomachus would have been pleased to have a son. Seven days after Aristotle's birth, there would have been a party. Garlands of olive leaves decorated the house, friends brought presents, and Nicomachus went to the temple to thank the gods for his new son.

Aristotle's home town

Like most Greek towns, Stagira had an open square, called the *agora*, used for markets and public meetings. Around this square were small houses with sloping roofs of reddish clay tiles, and elegant wood and stone temples. Doctor Nicomachus must have been a leading **citizen** in this small community.

► This picture from a wall-carving in Greece shows Asclepius, the god of healing, treating a man with a bad arm.

▲ Every Greek town had at least one temple, where people left gifts for the gods. This is the temple of the goddess Athena in the city of Delphi.

Medicine in Greece

Doctors in Greece practised a mixture of medicine and magic. The god of healing was Asclepius, and people prayed to him when they or their relatives were ill. Nicomachus gave his patients medicines made from herbs, and performed surgical operations, without painkilling drugs. He probably also knew of new ideas, put forward by a doctor named Hippocrates, who believed in practical cures based on knowing how the body worked.

Sons and daughters

Greek fathers welcomed a boy baby. A son would grow up to be a citizen, inherit the family property and support his ageing parents. A daughter could not do these things, for in Greece women did not have the same freedoms and rights as men.

Aristotle's childhood

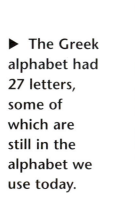

Nicomachus was rich, so Aristotle's mother had **slaves** as servants and a nurse to help look after her young son. Poor women went out often, to fetch **charcoal** for the cooking fire or water from the well, but the doctor's wife probably stayed at home most of the time. A rich woman ran her household, told the servants what to do, and made sure the family had enough clothes. Much of her time was spent spinning and weaving. She went out only to visit the temple, the hairdresser or perhaps a woman friend, and when she did, a slave usually went with her. Her husband ordered the shopping from the market, and the goods were delivered to the house. When Nicomachus attended a feast at the king's palace, his wife probably stayed at home. Respectable women did not go to parties.

A meeting with a prince

When Aristotle was three, his parents would have celebrated his birthday with prayers and a special meal. Little boys were given a present – a small decorated pottery jug, like those the men owned. By the time he was five, Aristotle probably had a **tutor**. He was an educated slave who taught the boy the letters of the Greek alphabet.

▶ The Greek alphabet had 27 letters, some of which are still in the alphabet we use today.

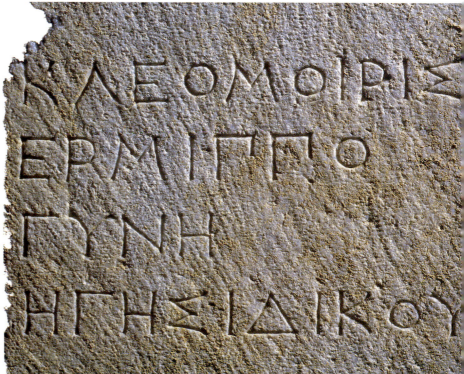

As Aristotle grew older, his father must have taken him to the king's court. King Amyntas had three sons, and the youngest was just two years younger than Aristotle. His name was Philip. He was probably already training to be a soldier. He admired the Spartans, the toughest soldiers in Greece. In any arguments, it's likely that Aristotle stuck up for the Athenians.

Athens and Sparta

Athens was the richest and most artistic of all the Greek cities. Sparta was the most warlike. The Spartans trained their boys for war. The Athenians had the best navy in Greece, but their leaders were as famous for making speeches as for fighting. Athenian **citizens governed** themselves. The Spartans, who disliked new ideas such as **democracy**, were ruled by a small group of warrior-nobles. Yet Spartan women could own their houses. Women in Athens could not.

▶ Greek children had many toys that are still familiar playthings today. This Greek doll has arms and legs that can move.

Children's toys

Children in Greece spent a lot of their time playing outdoors. They flew kites, played board games with dice, and had wooden and pottery dolls with painted faces, and jointed arms and legs. Babies had pottery potties and feeding cups, the same shapes as modern plastic ones.

Family life

Aristotle left no account of his childhood, but we can work out roughly what his early life would have been like from what **historians** and **archaeologists** have discovered about Greek family life.

A Greek house

Aristotle's home would have been a typical house of the time, made of stone, mud brick and timber, with a clay tile roof. An ancient Greek house had few windows on the outside walls, but did have an inner courtyard, cool and shaded in summer. Men and women had separate rooms in the house. Aristotle would have slept on a bed with ropes strung across a wooden frame. His few clothes and toys were probably stored in baskets or wooden chests.

Aristotle the animal-lover

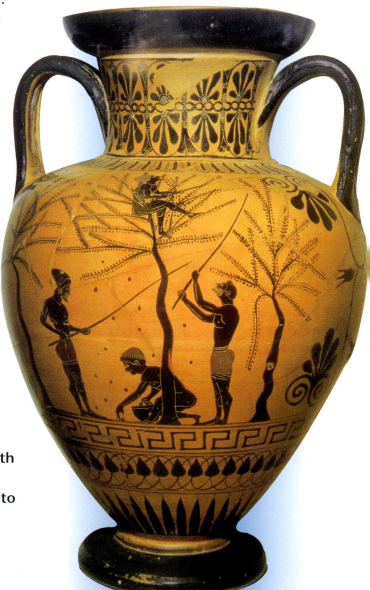

Many Greek children kept pets – cats, dogs, birds, tortoises, even snakes and lizards. Aristotle almost certainly had pets, for he loved nature. He probably also asked the mountain shepherds about the wolves, boar, deer and even the occasional lion they saw.

▶ The scene on this Greek vase shows the olive harvest. Men with long sticks are hitting the tree branches to make the olives fall to the ground.

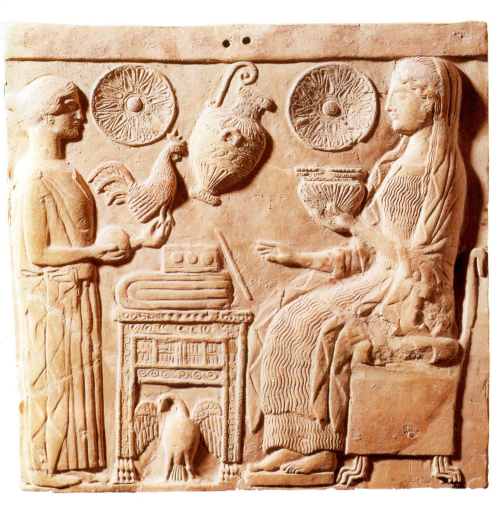

◄ A Greek woman wore a long linen dress, called a *chiton*, and put on a *himation*, partly covering her head, when she went out.

Clothes

As a child, Aristotle would have worn a short **tunic**, and run around barefoot. Young men wore short kilts or tunics made from wool or linen, but older men wore ankle-length tunics, sometimes with a cloak, called a *himation*, on top. **Slaves** and workers often wore just a **loincloth**.

Many Greeks were farmers. They grew barley and wheat for bread-making, and grapes for making wine. They also grew olives. These were eaten and also crushed for their oil. Oil was used in cooking and burned in clay lamps at night. There were lots of fishermen, too.

Meal times

For breakfast, Aristotle would have eaten bread soaked in wine or milk. Lunch would have been bread and cheese, with olives, grapes or figs. For their evening meal, people ate barley porridge, with beans, lettuce, cabbage, carrots and onions, and sometimes fish. Most Greeks only ate meat on feast-days.

Schooldays

Aristotle probably had his first lessons in science and medicine from his father. Doctors usually passed on their skills to their sons. Around the age of seven, Aristotle would have started school. In Greece, only boys from wealthy families went to school. Girls were taught at home by their mothers.

Greek schools

Most Greek schools had fewer than 20 pupils. The boys wrote on wooden tablets coated with wax, using a pointed stick called a stylus as a pen. They did sums moving beads on wire on a wooden frame called an abacus. Aristotle would also have studied history and learned parts of Homer's long poems by heart. He also knew the speeches of the famous Athenian leader, Pericles (490–429 BC).

At fourteen, Aristotle would have played sports well. He and his friends would practise on an open sanded field. They wrestled, ran races and threw the **javelin** and **discus**. The best athletes might take part in the **Olympic Games**, held every four years to honour Zeus, king of the gods.

▶ **This statue shows an athlete throwing the discus. Greek athletes did not wear clothes in races and other competitions.**

The theatre and friends

Most Greeks loved the theatre, and Aristotle would almost certainly have gone. Theatres were hollowed out of hillsides. The audience sat on stone benches arranged in rings down the hill. The stage was at the bottom. Masked actors performed comedies – funny plays – or sad, serious tragedies.

As he grew older, Aristotle would have shared the company of grown men who came to the house for dinner. Men did not eat with women. They lay on couches, talking while they ate with their fingers from dishes carried in by **slaves**, and drank wine.

▶ Greek actors wore masks. The expression on the mask showed the character's age and feelings. The large mouth helped to make the actor's voice louder.

Slaves and freemen

One in four people in Greece was a slave. Slaves were usually prisoners captured in war. They were sold or hired for work in the town market, but most were treated quite kindly. Slaves could be freed, and a few became wealthy businessmen.

The quest for knowledge

In 367 BC, when he was seventeen, Aristotle travelled south to Athens to go to **university**. His new school was called the Academy, and it was run by Greece's most famous teacher, Plato.

Life in Athens

Athens was the biggest and most beautiful city in Greece. Over it stood the hill called the Acropolis. On the hill top was the gleaming temple of the Parthenon. About 250,000 people lived in the city. It must have seemed to Aristotle that they spent most of their time talking about **politics**. A famous ruler of Athens, Pericles, once said that someone with no interest in politics had no business living in Athens!

A democratic city

Athens was not ruled by a king. It was a **democracy**, where the laws were made by an assembly of free men, called **citizens**. The citizens could vote to get rid of any **politician** who annoyed them! That person was then sent into **exile**.

◀ This picture shows pieces of broken pottery, called *ostraka*. Athenian citizens could vote for a politician they wanted to exile by writing his name on *ostraka*.

A brilliant student hears a lesson

Plato soon saw that Aristotle was his most brilliant student. The two must have argued for hours. Plato said that a picture of a table was not as good as a real table; Aristotle wanted to know how the table was made. Plato wanted to know about a person's **soul**. Aristotle was just as interested in what went on inside a person's stomach!

Plato no doubt offered his young friend good advice. He would have warned him that clever people often made powerful enemies. Plato's own teacher, Socrates, had been accused of dishonouring the gods. He was condemned to death and killed himself by drinking poison.

▲ This painting of 1510 by the Italian artist Raphael shows Plato and Aristotle (right) walking and talking together.

Plato

Plato's real name was Aristocles – 'Plato' was a nickname, meaning 'broad-shouldered'. Plato had left Athens in disgust after Socrates (469–399 BC) was sentenced to death. He returned in 387 BC and started the Academy, in a grove of trees. The Academy was like a very early university. Plato was 60 when Aristotle came to study with him.

A school of his own

For 20 years, Aristotle studied and worked in Plato's
school and the two men became close friends.
Plato was keenly interested in ideas and in questions of
right and wrong. Aristotle was more practical. He wanted
to learn about the natural world and how it worked. The two
clever friends argued about everything, from how a city should
be **governed** to why fish could not breathe out of water.

The student traveller

In the holidays, it's likely that Aristotle travelled around Greece,
usually on foot. As he wandered, he studied plants and animals,
listened to people's stories and observed the stars and the
changing seasons.

Leaving the Academy

Around 347 BC Plato died, aged 81. Aristotle wrote that Plato
had shown 'by his own life, how to be happy is to be good'.
The Academy was now to be run by Plato's nephew,
Speusippus. Aristotle, now 37, decided it was time to start a
school of his own.

◄ This Roman
mosaic shows a
scene at Plato's
Academy.

He sailed across the Aegean Sea to Asia Minor (modern Turkey), where two old student friends were living in a town named Assus. The local ruler, Hermeias of Atarneus, was a soldier who had made a fortune from gold mines. With money to spend on learning, he invited Aristotle to lead a new school in Assus.

Aristotle settled down happily. Hermeias became a student, a friend and, before long, his father-in-law, for Aristotle married Hermeias's adopted daughter, Pythias. The newly-weds soon had a daughter, whom they named Pythias, too.

▼ After Aristotle's wedding, there would have been a party. These servants are bringing in the food and drink for a feast.

Marriage in the Greek world

In Greece, girls married at fourteen or fifteen, but men often married late, like Aristotle. Perhaps he remembered Plato's warning that it was a crime for a man not to marry! Like most Greek men, Aristotle lived apart from his wife much of the time.

The fish in the sea

After his first wife died, we know that Aristotle married again. His new wife was called Herpyllis, and the couple had a son, named Nicomachus.

Three years after his arrival at Assus, Aristotle decided to spend some time on the island of Lesbos. He made the short voyage to the island in one of the many small ships that sailed the Aegean Sea. The sailors probably pointed out the landmarks they used to find their way, and the dolphins and turtles in the water.

Naturalist on the island

Lesbos had once been the home of Greece's best woman poet, Sappho. Aristotle enjoyed poetry and was developing his own ideas about how it should be written. But his main interest now was **biology**. For two summers he wandered the island as a **naturalist**.

Studying sea creatures

On Lesbos, Aristotle did what scientists today call 'field work'. He watched birds and insects, and wandered along the beaches, picking up shells and peering into pools for sea creatures. Perhaps he enjoyed trips in fishing boats, examining the fish in the nets. He made notes of everything he saw.

▶ This wall painting from the island of Thera (modern-day Santorini) shows a fisherman with his catch.

Aristotle saw that if scientists were to make sense of the natural world, they must look at everything in detail. Scientists must believe what they saw, not what people told them. He also wondered about life and death, and about the **soul**. Was it separate from the body, as Plato thought, or were body and soul linked in some mysterious way?

▲ Greek trading ships had one sail. Warships like this had a single sail but were also rowed by men pulling on long oars.

The Greeks at sea

Aristotle would have learned much about life at sea during his Aegean travels. The Greeks sailed in wooden ships, with a single mast and a square sail. Like other sea travellers, Aristotle probably wore his valuables in a bag around his neck, so that anyone finding his drowned body would pay for its burial.

A royal summons

Aristotle was dragged away from this pleasant life of research in 342 BC, when Hermeias received a message from Philip of Macedonia.

Philip plans to rule all Greece

Philip had become king of Macedonia in 359 BC, after the deaths of his elder brothers, Alexander and Perdiccas. He was planning to rule all of Greece, and wanted Hermeias to join him in fighting against **Persia**. By going to war, Philip hoped to unite all the Greeks under his leadership.

Philip also had a personal request. He and his queen, Olympias, had a son, Alexander. The teenage prince needed a **tutor**. Hermeias had recommended the cleverest teacher in Assus – Aristotle. Philip invited Aristotle to come to his court in Pella and teach his son. It was a summons that Aristotle could hardly refuse.

◀ This painted dish shows a Greek soldier called a hoplite. Hoplites wore armour made of metal and leather, a helmet and carried a round shield and a spear.

The journey to Pella

So Aristotle packed his notes and the baskets full of shells, dried starfish and pressed flowers that he had collected. He crossed the Aegean Sea once more, with his family and servants. They finished the journey on foot, with their belongings bumping along in a cart. Pella must have seemed a small, rough city to someone who had spent so long in Athens, but Aristotle received a warm welcome.

Alexander was 13 when Aristotle met him. Philip wanted his son to have the best education, but quickly. War was coming, and then Alexander would have to ride into battle alongside his father.

▶ Scientists at Manchester University made this model of King Philip's head, based on a skull found in his tomb. It shows the scar of an arrow wound.

Aristotle the teacher

Aristotle believed that education should 'mould' a child into a good **citizen**. Children should first be taught to be fit and athletic. Then they should study reading and writing, music, gymnastics, drawing and mathematics. Older students should study literature and geography, before going on to explore every kind of knowledge.

Teaching the great

For the next three years, the teenage prince and the middle-aged scientist worked together. Aristotle found Alexander an eager pupil, interested in **philosophy**, medicine and history. We can imagine him watching as Aristotle explained how caterpillars changed into butterflies, listening to Aristotle reading from Homer's *Iliad*, and puzzling over why shooting stars raced across the night sky.

Aristotle and Alexander

Eventually, the **tutor's** work was ended. Philip left his son in charge of Macedonia while he was away fighting, and Alexander became a soldier. After Philip's victory over Athens at the battle of Chaeronea in 338 BC, Macedonia controlled all of Greece.

In Athens, people feared their new ruler would end their freedom. Philip did not speak Greek well, so to the Athenians, he was at least half a **barbarian**, but the king respected Aristotle's wisdom. Aristotle probably helped to write the **treaty** with Athens, urging all Greeks to fight **Persia**, after the terrible news came that his friend Hermeias had been captured by the Persians and put to death.

▲ Homer's poem the *Iliad* tells the story of the Trojan War. This vase painting shows one of the heroes of the story, Achilles, killing the Amazon queen Penthesilea.

Advice to a future conqueror

Hermeias had died bravely, and Aristotle wrote a poem in his memory. He compared Hermeias to the hero Achilles. It is possible that he told Alexander to avenge his friend by overthrowing the king of Persia.

It is hard to tell how much Alexander followed what Aristotle taught him. Aristotle believed the Greek city-states should be free. Alexander became the all-powerful ruler of an **empire**. Aristotle thought Greek ways were better than those of barbarians, but Alexander came to admire and copy many Eastern customs.

▶ This marble **bust** is of Aristotle's most famous pupil, Alexander the Great. It is a Roman copy of a Greek statue.

How Greeks fought

Most Greek soldiers fought on foot, marching in a tight mass called a phalanx. Their weapons included a long spear, a **javelin** or throwing spear, a **bronze** sword, and a bow. The Macedonian army was particularly strong in horsemen.

War and peace

Aristotle and his household returned to his home town of Stagira around 339 BC. He was probably glad to be away from Pella, where there was trouble at the royal court.

Philip's death

In 337 BC King Philip divorced Queen Olympias, and married a new wife. This led to a furious quarrel between the king and Alexander. Then in 336 BC Philip was murdered – supposedly by a young noble, although some people accused Alexander of plotting his father's death. Aristotle did not think so. In his book *Politics*, he described Philip's death as an example of how a ruler might be removed by one man, acting on a personal grudge.

▲ This piece of a Roman mosaic shows Alexander (far left, on horseback) leading his army to victory over the Persian king, Darius III, at the Battle of Issus.

▲ Athens was the home of Greek **democracy**. Aristotle enjoyed teaching in the city but, like many important men, he had enemies there, too.

Alexander goes to war

In 335 BC Aristotle returned to Athens. He was nearly 50, and there was a lot of scientific work he wanted to finish. The new king, Alexander crushed a **revolt** in Thebes, but spared Athens, which had joined with Thebes in standing up for freedom. He visited the **oracle** at Delphi, where he was told that he would never be defeated. In 334 BC Alexander marched east with over 35,000 soldiers to conquer Asia.

Back in Athens

In Athens, Aristotle was friendly with a Macedonian general, Antipater, who was left in charge while Alexander was away. Among the men Alexander had taken with him to Asia was Callisthenes, Aristotle's nephew. In 328 BC Alexander accused Callisthenes of **treason** and had him killed. Such a wrong angered Aristotle.

Home in the city

City life suited Aristotle. He enjoyed browsing in Athens' book market, where **papyrus scrolls** of plays, speeches and poetry were sold. The city was full of life and ideas. Plato had written about an ideal city, but Aristotle thought that real cities showed human **civilization** at its best.

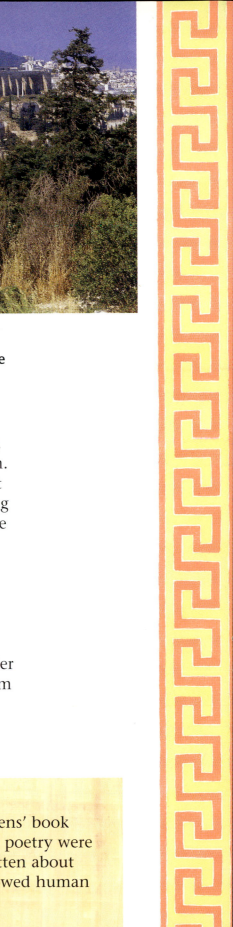

The Lyceum

The last thirteen years of Aristotle's life (335–322 BC) were spent setting up his own school in Athens. It was called the Lyceum. Its students met in a grove of trees just outside the city. Most of the writings by Aristotle that have lasted are notes of the **lectures** that he gave to his students, while walking beneath the trees.

The teachers and students ate together, argued, and read **scrolls** in the library, which had been paid for by Alexander.

The great man

Aristotle was now a great man in a city of great men. **Busts** and statues of him show someone who looks ready to talk **politics**, discuss poetry or explain why crabs have shells. He was wealthy and smartly dressed. He liked fine cloaks and rings.

◄ Aristotle and his students spent much of their time walking and discussing, like the **philosophers** on this Greek vase.

Aristotle leaves Athens and dies

Alexander had conquered an **empire** stretching as far as India, but in 323 BC he died suddenly in Babylon. The Greek world was thrown into turmoil. General Antipater was called away from Athens. Aristotle, 'the Macedonians' friend', became a target for hate. Aristotle feared he would meet the same fate as Socrates – death.

Aristotle and his wife fled to Chalcis, on the island of Euboea. He made his will, thanking his family for their love. He left instructions that his **slaves** be freed after his death, and that statues of the god Zeus and the goddess Athena be erected in his home town of Stagira. He began to complain of stomach pains, and in 322 BC he died, at the age of 62.

▲ The island of Euboea (also known as Evvia), just off the east coast of Greece, may have been Aristotle's burial place.

Aristotle's grave?

Aristotle's mother was born on the island of Euboea. In 1896, **archaeologists** working there found a **tomb** containing a skull, seven gold diadems (head-bands), two styluses, a pen, and a small clay statue of a man. The tomb may have been Aristotle's, or have some link with his family.

What Aristotle left to the world

Aristotle passed on much of what Greeks before him had thought, and added many more of his own ideas. Only parts of his last great work, *On Philosophy*, remain, but it has probably affected Western thought more than any other book of **philosophy**. Other titles of books by Aristotle show how widely he thought: *Physics*, about why things change; *On the Soul*, about the **soul** and the body; *Metaphysics* about religion; *Poetics* about literature; *Politics* about **government**.

Interested in everything

Aristotle was interested in everything. He made lists of the winners of the **Olympic Games**, the best plays, the forms of government in Greek cities. He wrote about '**barbarian** customs' and put together an **encyclopedia** of natural history.

He asked questions such as 'why is the sea salty?' and 'why does hitting a ball of wool make less sound than hitting a metal plate?' He tried to answer these questions from what he saw. This was an important lesson for future scientists.

◀ **This Roman statue shows Aristotle thinking. Of his hundreds of books, only 47 are now known.**

How Aristotle's ideas survived

After Aristotle's death, the Lyceum continued. One story tells how Aristotle's books passed to a friend, and ended up in a mouldy cellar. In about 60 BC, Andronicus of Rhodes, the last head of the Lyceum, rescued and published them.

The Romans admired Aristotle greatly, but from AD 500–1100 he was almost forgotten in Europe. Then in 1204, **crusaders** from Europe captured the city of Constantinople (modern Istanbul, in Turkey), and brought home copies of Aristotle's works. In this way, Aristotle was rediscovered by the West.

For a long time, Aristotle ruled the world of knowledge. His ideas were the basis for all science. His ideas on drama were held up as rules for writing plays. Today, Aristotle is no longer so important, but his ideas are at the base of the way people in the West think, and of many of the things they do.

▲ Aristotle's ideas were studied in the Arab world. This picture from a Turkish manuscript, from the 13th century AD, shows Aristotle (right) teaching some students science.

Glossary

archaeologist someone who studies the past from its remains, such as objects found beneath the ground or under the sea

barbarian to the Greeks, anyone who spoke a foreign language

biology scientific study of living things

bronze mixture of the metals copper and tin

bust statue of a person's head and shoulder's

charcoal special burnt wood, used as fuel

citizen free man, who could help govern a Greek city-state

civilization highly developed society

colony settlement founded by Greeks in another country

conqueror ruler who seizes other lands or peoples by force

court physician doctor who works for a ruler in the ruler's palace

crusaders European soldiers who fought in the Holy Land (Palestine) during the Middle Ages

democracy 'rule by the people', a political system in which everyone has a say in the government

discus saucer-shaped object, thrown by an athlete

encyclopedia book or books containing information about one or many subjects

empire several countries all ruled by one person

exile being forced to leave one's home to live abroad

government the way a place or people is ruled, or governed

historian someone who studies and writes about the past

javelin spear thrown by a soldier or athlete

loincloth short piece of cloth that hangs from the waist

naturalist someone who studies animals and plants

Olympic Games in Ancient Greece, a festival of sports and arts held to honour the gods

oracle sacred place where the Greeks went to consult a god or goddess about their future fate

papyrus kind of paper made from reeds, invented in Egypt

Persia country in Asia (modern Iran)

philosopher thinker who tries to understand the universe and human life. The word 'philosopher' means 'someone who loves knowledge' in Greek.

politicians person whose job involves government

politics the business of government

revolt rising by people against their rulers

scroll ancient book, made from a long roll of papyrus or animal skin (parchment), wrapped around two wooden sticks

slave servant who was the property of his master or mistress

soul part of a person that many people believe causes us to think or behave as we do. In some religions, the soul is believed to live on after the body dies.

tomb burial place, often marked by a stone or a building

treason crime of plotting against a ruler or government

treaty agreement made between states

tunic loose garment, reaching to just above the knee, often sleeveless

tutor teacher hired for a child at home

university place where many subjects are taught at an advanced level

Timeline

850 BC	Famous Greek poet, Homer, probably alive around this time
776 BC	First known Olympic Games
550 BC	Cyrus the Great founds the Persian Empire
500–449 BC	Greeks at war with Persian invaders
480–431 BC	So-called 'Golden Age' in Greece; Pericles leads Athens
431–404 BC	Peloponnesian War between Athens and Sparta: Sparta wins
399 BC	Death of the philosopher Socrates
384 BC	Aristotle is born in Stagira, in northeastern Greece
367 BC	Aristotle travels to Athens to study with Plato
347 BC	Plato dies
344 BC	Aristotle studies nature on the island of Lesbos
338 BC	Philip of Macedonia rules all Greece
336 BC	Philip dies, and his son Alexander becomes king of Greece
335 BC	Aristotle founds the Lyceum school in Athens
323 BC	Death of Alexander the Great
322 BC	Aristotle dies
146 BC	The Romans conquer Greece
AD 750	Arabs spread the religion of Islam, and preserve the writings of Aristotle in the East
AD 1200s	Crusaders bring Aristotle's ideas from the East to western Europe

Further reading & websites

Digging Deeper into the Past: The Greeks, John and Louise James, Heinemann Library, 1997

Focus On History: Ancient Greeks, Anita Ganeri, Franklin Watts, 2001

Heinemann Explore History: Ancient Greece, Jane Shuter, Heinemann Library, 2001

How Would You Survive as an Ancient Greek? Fiona Macdonald, Franklin Watts, 1995

Sightseers: Ancient Greece, Julie Ferris, Heinemann Library, 2000

Heinemann Explore – an online resource from Heinemann.
For key stage 2 history go to *www.heinemannexplore.com*
www.pbs.org/empires/thegreeks

Places to visit

British Museum, London

All the Internet addresses (URLs) given in this book were valid at the time of going to press. However, due to the dynamic nature of the Internet, some addresses may have changed, or sites may have ceased to exist since publication. While the author and publishers regret any inconvenience this may cause readers, no responsibility for any such changes can be accepted by either the author or the publishers.

Index

Titles in the Life and World of series include:

The Life and World of
ARISTOTLE
Brian Williams

Hardback   0 431 14765 5

The Life and World of
BOUDICCA
Struan Reid

Hardback   0 431 14771 X

The Life and World of
CLEOPATRA
Struan Reid

Hardback   0 431 14774 4

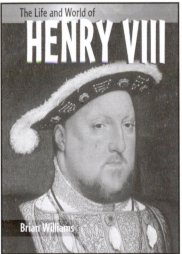

The Life and World of
HENRY VIII
Brian Williams

Hardback   0 431 14767 1

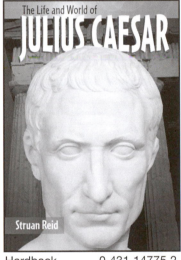

The Life and World of
JULIUS CAESAR
Struan Reid

Hardback   0 431 14775 2

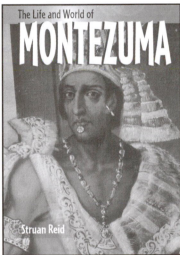

The Life and World of
MONTEZUMA
Struan Reid

Hardback   0 431 14763 9

The Life and World of
QUEEN VICTORIA
Brian Williams

Hardback   0 431 14769 8

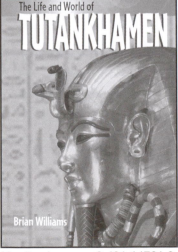

The Life and World of
TUTANKHAMEN
Brian Williams

Hardback   0 431 14761 2

Find out about the other titles in this series on our website www.heinemann.co.uk/library